DMT

The Beginners Introductory Guide to Dimethyltryptamine + How to Have the Best DMT Experience

By Psychedelic Academy

Copyright © 2021. All Right Reserved. All rights reserved. No part of this guide may be reproduced in any form without permission in writing from the publisher except in the case of brief quotations embodied in critical articles or reviews.

Legal & Disclaimer

The information contained in this book and its contents is not designed to replace or take the place of any form of medical or professional advice. It is not meant to replace the need for independent medical, financial, legal, or other professional advice or services, as may be required. The content and information in this book have been provided for educational and entertainment purposes only.

The content and information contained in this book have been compiled from sources deemed reliable, and it is accurate to the best of the Author's knowledge, information, and belief. However, the author cannot guarantee its accuracy and validity and cannot be held liable for any errors and omissions. Further, changes are periodically made to this book as and when needed. Where appropriate and necessary, you must consult a professional (including but not limited to your doctor, attorney, financial advisor, or such other professional advisor) before using any of the suggested remedies, techniques, or information in this book.

Upon using the contents and information contained in this book, you agree to hold harmless the Author from and against any damages, costs, and expenses, including any legal fees potentially resulting from the application of any of the information provided by this book. This disclaimer applies to any loss, damages or injury caused by the use and application, whether directly or indirectly, of any advice or information presented, whether for breach of contract, tort, negligence, personal injury, criminal intent, or under any other cause of action.

You agree to accept all risks of using the information presented inside this book.

You agree that by continuing to read this book, where appropriate and necessary, you shall consult a professional (including but not limited to your doctor, attorney, or financial advisor or such other advisor as needed) before using any of the suggested remedies, techniques, or information in this book.

TABLE OF CONTENTS

INTRODUCTIO

CHAPTER 1: HALLUCINOGENS

DEPENDENCE AND ADDICTION TO HALLUCINOGENIC DRUGS

THE EFFECTS OF HALLUCINOGENS ON THE BRAIN

CHAPTER 2: DRUG ADDICTION AND ABUSE

CHAPTER 3: PSYCHEDELICS

AYAHUASCA

PSILOCYBIN MUSHROOMS

PSYCHEDELICS AS MEDICINE

EARLY PSYCHEDELIC RESEARCH

LONG-TERM STIGMA

THE SOCIETAL EFFECTS OF PSYCHEDELICS

CHAPTER 4: DIMETHYLTYPTAMINE (DMT)

WHAT ARE DMT'S SIDE EFFECTS?

WHAT ARE THE DMT RISKS?

SHORT-TERM EFFECTS OF DMT

EFFECTS OF DMT ABUSE IN THE LONG TERM

ADDICTION TO DMT

TREATMENT FOR DMT ADDICTION

DMT STAYS IN YOUR SYSTEM FOR HOW LONG?

HOW TO REMOVE DMT FROM YOUR SYSTEM

CHAPTER 5: DMT EXTRACTION

CHAPTER 6: EGO DEATH

THE EGO'S STRUCTURAL ELEMENTS

MOMENTS BEYOND THE EGO

EGO DEATH AND PSYCHEDELIC THERAPY

THREE THINGS TO THINK ABOUT BEFORE TAKING DMT

UNDERSTANDING THE EXPERIENCE OF AN ACID TRIP.

THE DIFFERENCE BETWEEN A GOOD AND A BAD TRIP

EXTRACTION OF DMT

A STEP-BY-STEP TUTORIAL TO EXTRACTING DMT

THE SHORT VERSION ADAPTED

INTRODUCTION

Although hallucinogens (psychedelics) have been in the human pharmacopeia for millennia, the molecular mechanisms that alter perception and consciousness so profoundly remain a mystery. It is the only type of chemical that does so effectively and specifically. Humans also don't fully comprehend "perception biochemistry" or how we may have such a rich and complex interior life without external inputs. We don't understand the basic physiological mechanisms that underpin some of our most typical experiences, such as the many human attributes of creativity, imagination, and dream states. This is true for atypical states of consciousness such as "visions" or uncontrolled hallucinations, as well as events such as near-death encounters (NDE). And it's a concern that, despite the importance of these fields in the growth of our science, psychology, philosophy, and society, we haven't applied the scientific method to them enough.

The effects of hallucinogens are frequently linked to dreamlike states. The effects of prescribed hallucinogenic medications, on the other hand, are significantly more powerful, intense, and overwhelming than mere dreams.

Chapter 1: HALLUCINOGENS

Psychoactive chemicals known as hallucinogens affect one's perception of reality. Hallucinogens, often known as psychedelic chemicals, allow people to experience feelings, see, or hear things that aren't there or alter their view of the world around them. Some work right away, while others take a little longer. Being under the effect of a psychedelic is referred to as tripping. PCP (phencyclidine, or "angel dust"), LSD (lysergic acid diethylamide), and ketamine are examples of hallucinogens that can be manufactured. Others are substances found in nature, such as those found in certain plants. The peyote cactus produces the psychedelic mescaline, while psilocybin is found in certain fungi known as "magic mushrooms."

Hallucinogens come in different forms.

Hallucinogens are available in different forms. Example:

•LSD is commonly consumed as gelatine soaked in LSD or little squares of blotting paper and then swallowed, but it can also be taken as pills or tablets.

- PCP is usually sold in capsules, tablets, or powders in a variety of colors. It is usually smoked, although it can also be snorted, swallowed, or injected.

- Medical professionals and veterinarians utilize ketamine as an esthetic. It's a psychedelic substance that's commonly used illegally. It can be dissolved in fluids or formed into tablets or pills. It's commonly taken by mouth, injected, or snorted.

- Mescaline is a white powder derived from the peyote cactus, while dried, pulverized peyote buttons are available in capsule form. It's commonly taken by mouth, although it can also be chewed or smoked.

- Magic mushrooms can be either be consumed cooked, fresh or boiled into a drink.

- Ayahuasca is a psychedelic tea made from plants. Ayahuasca is a South American plant that has gained popularity among western travelers.

Some depressant and stimulant substances, such as cannabis and ecstasy, can cause hallucinations in large doses. Unintentional death is a serious concern when hallucinogens cause a person's sense of time, space, and objective reality to be skewed.

Hallucinogens that have been produced are known as synthetic hallucinogens.

In recent years, various synthetic products purporting to have hallucinogenic properties have become accessible in Australia. A variety of compounds could be used as the active ingredient in these goods. NBOMes and PMA are examples of synthetic hallucinogens frequently advertised as other pharmaceuticals yet contain quite different components, resulting in potentially hazardous and unexpected consequences.

What are hallucinogens, and how do they work?

Hallucinogens modify the brain's perception of sensory information by affecting certain areas of the brain. An individual might be staring at a blank wall, but their hallucinating brain may see it moving and swirling or covered in insects.

Various hallucinogens have different effects.

The effects of hallucinogens vary based on the type of substance, the dose intensity, and the individual's mental state and functionality.

The following are some of the most prevalent hallucinogen side effects:

- sensations, such as colors being "heard" or sounds being "felt."
- a sense of disconnection from one's body
- a faster heart rate
- relaxation
- pupils that are dilated
- nauseousness and a lack of appetite
- direction, time, and distance distortions
- sound, sight, taste, and touch hallucinations Bad trips and hallucinogens

Hallucinogens are a highly unpredictable class of medications. Just because someone has a good time on their first trip doesn't mean they will have a good time every time.

Everyone is in danger of having a "bad trip." Symptoms include nightmares, horrific hallucinations, paranoia, and nausea. On a single journey, it is also possible to have a mix of negative and positive experiences.

Other unfavorable impacts may include:

- Muscular spasms and coordination problems

- Unconsciousness and convulsions

- Angry, aggressive, and violent behavior

- Catatonic condition, which causes the person to become 'zombie-like.'

If you suspect an overdose, dial triple zero (000) immediately for an ambulance.

Individuals use phrases like tolerance, reliance, and withdrawal to express how they feel.

Tolerance to hallucinogens, like many other drugs, can be established. This means that higher and larger doses are required to get the same effect.

Some people develop a psychological dependence on drugs and believe that consuming them on a regular basis is an essential part of their lives. According to studies, hallucinogens like PCP or ketamine can cause physical addiction. If a person stops taking their drug, they may have withdrawal symptoms.

Long-term psychedelic use can cause harm.

Some people may have 'flashbacks,' which can occur days, weeks, months, or even years after taking the medication. They may encounter distortions of their current reality or relive the hallucinations of a prior trip so vividly that it appears as if they have been transported back in time and space.

Experiencing hallucinations without being on any hallucinogenic substances might be terrifying.

Treatment for drug addiction

Detoxification, individual counseling, and group therapy are all possibilities for treating drug addiction. For assistance and referrals, consult your doctor, or contact local alcohol and other drug treatment program.

Hallucinogens are drugs that affect the user's processes and perspective, causing significant distortions in reality. Many other types of pharmaceuticals have a different effect on one's perspective than these medications. The results of these drugs are interpreted by many as indicating new and even prolonged states of consciousness.

Some people experience synesthesia as a result (mixed sensory experiences, such as hearing colors or seeing sounds). Side effects of these medications include a distorted sense of time, hallucinations, and dissociative experiences (not feeling connected to one's body or reality).

Hallucinogen Abuse is a term used to describe the use of hallucinogens.

Because nearly all of the drugs mentioned above are prohibited (and the most strictly restricted), even minor use can be dangerous. Misuse of these medications can be

extremely dangerous to the user and those around them, and in certain situations, sustained abuse can develop into physical or psychological addiction.

DEPENDENCE AND ADDICTION TO HALLUCINOGENIC DRUGS

Even though addiction to hallucinogens is less prevalent

than other drugs, many people can depend on them. Tolerance to the drug is a sign of physical addiction, which means that more of the substance is required to produce the same high as before. When you quit using it, you'll notice that you're having withdrawal symptoms.

It is possible to develop a psychological dependency if:

•The user feels compelled to take the drug on a more regular basis.

•The user goes to great lengths to obtain the drug.

•The user begins to avoid duties and friends and family to focus on the substance.

•The user continues to use the substance even though he or she is aware of the serious implications of doing so.

Addiction to a mind-altering substance has been related to a variety of other illnesses, including depression.

For thousands of years, hallucinogenic chemicals found in mushrooms and plants (or their derivatives) have been used in religious rites. Because they include nitrogen, almost all hallucinogens are classified as alkaloids. Many hallucinogens have chemical structures similar to natural neurotransmitters (e.g., serotonin-, acetylcholine-, or catecholamine-like). While the exact mechanisms by which hallucinogens cause their effects are unknown, research suggests that they work by interfering with neurotransmitter activation or binding to receptor sites, at least in part. The following are four types of hallucinogens that will be discussed in this book:

LSD is one of the most potent mood-altering substances (d-lysergic acid diethylamide). It was discovered in 1938 and is manufactured from lysergic acid, which is found in ergot, a fungus that grows on rye and other cereals.

Peyote is a small, spineless cactus that contains the active ingredient mescaline. This plant has been used in religious rites by indigenous peoples in the southwest United States and northern Mexico. Mescaline can also be made through chemical synthesis.

Psilocybin (4-phosphoryloxy-N, N-dimethyltryptamine) is a hallucinogenic drug generated from mushrooms in Mexico, South America, and the United States. Psilocin and Psilocybin, another psychedelic, are normally present in trace amounts in these mushrooms.

In the 1950s, PCP (phencyclidine) was developed as an intravenous anesthetic. Its use has been discontinued due to serious adverse effects.

What are some of the ways hallucinogens are abused?

Hallucinogens have been propagated as drugs of abuse due to the same features that lead to their adoption into ritualistic or spiritual traditions. Unlike most other drugs, hallucinogens have a wide range of inconsistent effects, generating different effects in different people at different times. The amount and content of active compounds in hallucinogens derived from plants and mushrooms differ significantly. Because of their unexpected nature, hallucinogen use can be particularly dangerous.

LSD is normally taken orally and comes in tablets, capsules, and, on rare occasions, liquid. LSD is often mixed with absorbent paper and cut into ornamental pieces, each holding one dose. The adventures, which are frequently referred to as "trips," typically last 12 hours.

PEYOTE. The crown, or top, of the peyote cactus, is made up of disc-shaped buttons that have been dried after being detached from the roots. These buttons are usually eaten or soaked in water to generate an intoxicating drink. Mescaline has a hallucinogenic dose of 0.3 to 0.5 grams and has a 12-hour duration of action. Because the extract is bitter, some people prefer to prepare tea by boiling the cacti for several hours.

PSILOCYBIN. Psilocybin-containing mushrooms can be bought fresh or dried, and they're commonly taken by mouth. Psilocybin (4-phosphoryloxy-N, N-dimethyltryptamine) and its biologically active product, psilocin, are not inactivated by cooking or freezing (4-hydroxy-N, N-dimethyltryptamine). As a result, people can use it to brew tea or disguise other foods' bitterness. Psilocybin's effects last roughly 6 hours and appear within 20 minutes of ingestion.

PCP is a white crystalline powder that dissolves quickly in water or alcohol. It has a chemically bitter taste to it. PCP is easily dyed and sold on the black market in various tablet, pill, and colored powder forms that can be smoked snorted, or eaten orally. PCP is usually applied to a leafy material like mint, parsley, oregano, or marijuana for smoking. Depending on how much and taken, PCP's effects might last anywhere from 4 to 6 hours.

THE EFFECTS OF HALLUCINOGENS ON THE BRAIN

LSD, peyote, psilocybin, and PCP are hallucinogens that cause significant distortions in a person's perception of reality. People who use hallucinogens experience sights, sounds, and feelings that appear real but aren't. Several hallucinogens cause rapid, strong mood swings as a side effect. LSD, psilocybin, and peyote function by changing the way serotonin interacts with nerve cells.

The serotonin system affects perceptual, behavioral, and regulatory processes such as appetite, mood, body temperature, muscular control, sexual behavior, and sensory perception. It is present throughout the spinal cord and brain. PCP, on the other hand, acts on a glutamate receptor in the brain that is involved in pain perception, learning, memory, and environmental responses.

There has been no well-controlled research on the effects of these medications on the brain, but smaller research and case reports that highlight some of the negative effects of hallucinogen use have been published.

LSD. Sensations and feelings change far more dramatically than physical indications in people under the influence of LSD. Multiple emotions may be experienced simultaneously, or the person may jump from one to the next swiftly. When taken in big enough doses, the drug creates visual hallucinations and delusions. The user's sense of self-awareness and the passage of time is influenced. Experiences can "cross over" other senses, giving the user the impression of hearing sounds and seeing colors. These changes can be concerning, and they may cause you to be concerned. Some people have intense, dreadful feelings and thoughts of despair, dread of losing control, or fear of going insane and dying when using LSD.

LSD users may suffer flashbacks or recurrences of certain aspects of their drug experience. Flashbacks can occur suddenly and without warning, anywhere from a few days to more than a year after using LSD. Flashbacks continue and cause considerable distress or impairment in social or vocational functioning in some people with hallucinogen-induced persistent perceptual disorder (HPPD).

The majority of LSD users gradually lessen or stop using the drug over time. Because it does not generate compulsive drug-seeking, LSD is not classed as an addictive substance. Because LSD creates tolerance, frequent users will need to take increasingly higher doses to get the same level of intoxication as before. This is an extremely dangerous technique due to the medication's unpredictability. Cross-tolerance between LSD and other hallucinogens has also been discovered.

PEYOTE. Mescaline, the major active ingredient of peyote, has uncertain long-term psychological and cognitive effects. Native Americans who ingest peyote regularly in a religious setting have no cognitive or psychological impairments. However, it should be noted that these findings may not apply to people who use the drug recreationally regularly. Peyote users may also have flashbacks.

•PSILOCYBIN. Active compounds in psilocybin-containing "magic" mushrooms exhibit LSD-like properties and cause alterations in autonomic function, behavior, motor reflexes, and perception. Some of the psychological effects of psilocybin

use include hallucinations, a shift in temporal perception, and an inability to discern fantasy from reality. Other possible side effects include panic attacks and insanity, especially if a large amount is eaten. Long-term effects such as flashbacks, the danger of memory loss, psychiatric disorder, and tolerance have been recorded in case studies.

•PCP. When patients recovered from the anesthetic effects of PCP, they became confused, angry, and irrational; as a result, it was removed from the list of approved anesthetics in humans in 1965. PCP is a "dissociative drug," meaning it induces emotions of separation (dissociation) from the self and environment by distorting sound, vision, and perceptions. When PCP was first marketed as a street drug in the 1960s, it gained a reputation as a substance that might cause catastrophic reactions and was not worth the risk. Some abusers, on the other hand, continue to use PCP because it provides them feelings of power, strength, and invulnerability, as well as a mind-numbing effect. Some of the negative psychological effects that have been described include:

•Symptoms of schizophrenia include delusions, paranoia, hallucinations, disordered thinking, and a sense of being cut off from one's environment.

•Anxiety symptoms: About half of patients treated to emergency rooms for PCP- related problems (within the last 48 hours) report significant elevations in anxiety symptoms.

•People who have taken PCP for a long time have reported memory loss, speech and reasoning difficulties, melancholy, and weight loss. After you stop using PCP, you may experience these symptoms for up to a year.

Despite substantial negative consequences, PCP is addictive, and chronic use can lead to cravings and obsessive PCP-seeking behavior.

What other negative health impacts do hallucinogens have?

It is not rare for psychedelic use to cause unpleasant side effects. This could be owing to the enormous variety of psychoactive compounds found in any given hallucinogen source.

The dosage mostly determines LSD's effects. Dilated pupils and elevated body temperature, heart rate, and blood pressure are all symptoms of LSD use. It can also produce tremors, sleeplessness, excessive sweating, dry mouth, and a lack of appetite.

PEYOTE. Increased heart rate, body temperature, uncoordinated movements (ataxia), flushing, and excessive sweating are possible adverse effects. In at least one case, the active ingredient, mescaline, has been related to fetal abnormalities.

PSILOCYBIN. Side effects include muscle relaxation or weakness, vomiting, excessive pupil dilation, ataxia, nausea, and drowsiness. If one of the many deadly mushrooms is incorrectly classified as a psilocybin mushroom, people who ingest it risk becoming poisoned.

PCP. PCP produces a large increase in blood pressure,

pulse rate, and a modest increase in breathing rate at low-to-moderate doses. There may be excessive perspiration, flushing numbness in the extremities, and a lack of motor coordination as breathing becomes shallow.

At high doses, blood pressure, pulse rate, and respiration all drop. Symptoms include vomiting, nausea, eye flipping up and down, blurred vision, drooling, dizziness, and loss of balance. PCP abusers frequently end up in emergency rooms due to overdose or the drug's severe psychiatric side effects. While drunk, PCP users might become suicidal or violent, endangering themselves and others. High doses of PCP have been associated with coma, seizures, and death (though death more often results from accidental injury or suicide during PCP intoxication). Because of its sedative effects, PCP can cause coma when combined with other CNS depressants like benzodiazepines and alcohol.

Chapter 2: DRUG ADDICTION AND ABUSE

Addiction to drugs has far-reaching societal ramifications. The economic effect is expected to be over $215 billion, including everything from lost wages to legal, medical, and mental health consequences. Marijuana cultivation and synthetic drug production, such as methamphetamine, significantly impact soil and water supplies. Drug law violations are a common reason for arrests in the United States, with over 1.5 million arrests made in 2016.

Prescription drug abuse is on the rise among teenagers, particularly with narcotics (commonly referred to as opioids) and stimulant medicines (which doctors prescribe to alleviate acute pain) (which treat diseases including narcolepsy and attention deficit disorder).

Individuals with both a serious mental health problem and a drug abuse illness are referred to as "dual diagnoses." Substance abuse problems are unfortunately very common in people who are also suffering from a significant mental disease. Patients with dual diagnoses are also more prone to be noncompliant with their treatment.

- Unfortunately, drug abuse is fairly common, affecting approximately 8% of people in the United States at some point in their lives.

- Addiction and drug abuse, also known as drug use or substance disorder, is a self-destructive pattern of substance use that leads to significant problems and distress, such as tolerance or withdrawal from the substance.

- A person with a dual diagnosis has a substance addiction problem and a serious mental health problem.

- When consumed, people can abuse practically any chemical that gives them a euphoric ("high") feeling.

- Inhalants and household cleaners are two of the most commonly misused substances.

- While drug use disorder's psychological and physical effects vary depending on the substance, the overall impact of any drug-related substance use disorder can be devastating.

- Although there is no single cause for drug use disorders, psychological, biological, and social risk factors can all contribute to the development.

- While the effects of drugs on the brain differ based on the drug, almost every substance used impacts the executive functions of the brain, drugs impair the brain's ability to suppress acts that would otherwise be postponed or prevented.

- Recurrent drug use that results in legal problems occurs in potentially dangerous situations, interferes with necessary obligations, causes relationship or social or problems, withdrawal symptoms, tolerance, using a lot of the drug or for a long period, persistent desire to use the drug, unsuccessful attempts to stop using the drug, neglecting other responsibilities are all symptoms of a drug problem.

- Since no test can conclusively diagnose someone with a substance use disorder, health care providers assess these disorders by gathering family, comprehensive medical, and mental health data and obtaining a physical examination and lab tests to assess the patient's medical condition.

- The majority of people who suffer from substance abuse disorders do not take advantage of the treatment options that are accessible to them.

- The main aims of treatment are relapse prevention, sobriety, and rehabilitation

- Recovery from psychological addiction can be much more difficult and time- consuming than recovery from physical addiction.

- A person suffering from chemical dependency may require detoxification treatment during the early stages of sobriety to avoid or decrease withdrawal effects.

- Dual diagnosis therapy is more effective when the sufferer's mental illness is treated concurrently with substance dependency.

- There are times of drug-free living (remission) and periods of relapse when recovering from a substance use disorder.

- If left untreated, drug addiction increases the likelihood of a variety of undesirable life pressures and conditions.

What are the most often abused drugs?

Almost every drug that provides a euphoric ("high") experience when eaten can be abused. While most people are aware of the abuse of legal substances such as marijuana or alcohol (in most states) and cocaine, few are aware that inhalants such as household cleaners and over-the-counter medications such as cold treatments are also commonly abused. The following are some of the medications and types of pharmaceuticals that people commonly abuse and/or become dependent on:

•Amphetamines: This category of drugs includes prescription prescriptions including methylphenidate (Concerta, Ritalin, Focalin), dextroamphetamine, and

amphetamine (Adderall), as well as illegally manufactured narcotics like methamphetamine ("crystal meth"). Excessive consumption of any of these compounds can result in seizures and death.

•Alcohol: Despite being legal, alcohol is a harmful toxin, particularly for a growing fetus when a mother consumes it while pregnant. Alcoholism, one of the most frequent addictions, can have serious consequences for an alcoholic's physical well-being and his or her ability to function socially and at work.

•Anabolic steroids: Bodybuilders and other athletes are the most common users of this class of drugs, which can bring horrible emotional symptoms like paranoia and aggression, as well as serious long-term health consequences, including infertility and organ failure.

•Caffeine: While many people consume caffeine in tea, coffee, and soda, too much of it can cause palpitations, insomnia, tremors, irritability, and anxiety.

•Cathinones (bath salts): Cathinones are stimulant substances similar to cocaine, amphetamines, and Ecstasy. They are chemically unrelated to bath salts that people use to bathe (MDMA). Other street names for cathinones include "plant food," "jewelry cleanser," and "phone screen cleaning," among others.

•Cannabis (tetrahydrocannabinol): Tetrahydrocannabinol is the scientific name for cannabis, also known as marijuana (THC). Marijuana is the most commonly used illicit drug, with over 14 million people aged 12 and up admitting to consuming it in the preceding year. Marijuana is frequently blended (cut) with other narcotics so that drug lords can earn more profit selling the diluted drug or expose the consumer to more addictive drugs, exposing the user to the dangers connected with those addictive drugs. Marijuana is commonly cut with oregano, baby powder, embalming fluid, opiates, phencyclidine (PCP), and cocaine.

•Ecstasy: Because of its chemical properties (methylenedioxymethamphetamine), this substance is also known as MDMA (methylenedioxymethamphetamine). It causes euphoria and a growing desire or love to nurture others. If consumed in excess, it can raise body temperature to the point of death.

•Cocaine: Cocaine is a stimulant of the nervous system that can be inhaled as a powder, smoked in rocks ("crack"), or injected as a liquid.

Hallucinogens include drugs like LSD and mescaline, as well as so-called naturally occurring hallucinogens like mushrooms. These drugs can be hazardous since they tend to alter the user's perceptions. For example, a person high on a hallucinogen may see danger when none exists and assume that dangerous situations do not exist.

These misunderstandings can lead to dangerous behavior (like jumping out of a window because they think they have wings and can fly).

•Inhalants: Inhalants are widely found in home cleaners, such as ammonia, bleach, and other fume-emitting compounds. They are among the most commonly abused substances due to their simple accessibility. Using an inhalant even once or over some time might cause brain damage to the point of death, depending on the individual.

•Sedative, antianxiety or hypnotic pharmaceuticals: These compounds calm or depress the nervous system, making them the second most often used class of illicit narcotics. They can thus cause death by halting the person's breathing (respiratory arrest) who either overdoses on these medicines or mixes one or more of them with another nervous system depressant (like alcohol, another sedative drug, or an opiate).

•Opiates: Also known as narcotics or opioids, this class of medications includes heroin, methadone, hydrocodone, codeine, morphine, Percocet, Vicodin, OxyContin, and Percodan. This group of molecules has a big influence on how well the nervous system works. The lethality of opioids is frequently the result of the abuser having to use increasingly higher dosages to achieve the same level of intoxication, finally reaching a point where the amount required to get high is the same as the dose required to stop breathing by overdose (respiratory arrest).

•Nicotine: Nicotine, the addictive component present in cigarettes, is one of the most addictive drugs on the planet. Nicotine addiction is frequently compared to the strong addictiveness seen with opiates such as heroin.

•Phencyclidine: Also known as PCP, this substance can make the user feel suspicious, aggressive, and possess unusual physical power. This can make the individual extremely harmful to others.

What are the physical and psychological ramifications of

drug and alcohol abuse?

While the physical and psychological consequences of drug use disorders vary depending on the substance, the overall impact of drug addiction can be disastrous. Euphoria (as with Ecstasy, alcohol, or inhalant intoxication), paranoia (as with steroid or marijuana intoxication), extreme depression (as with amphetamine withdrawal or cocaine), or suicidal thoughts can all result from intoxication with or withdrawal from a substance (as with amphetamine withdrawal or cocaine). In terms of physical intoxication, the effects of a drug might range from sleep and slower breathing, as with sedative-hypnotic drugs or heroin, to a rapid heart rate, tremors, or cocaine intoxication, and seizures as with alcohol withdrawal.

What elements and causes contribute to the development of a substance addiction disorder?

Like most other mental health conditions, drug use problems have no one etiology and are not caused by a lack of discipline or self-control. Several psychological, biological, and social elements known as risk factors might enhance an individual's sensitivity to developing a chemical use disorder. In certain families, the prevalence of substance use problems appears to be higher than may be explained by the family's addictive environment. As a result, most substance abuse professionals understand that drug addiction is inherited.

Addiction and substance usage are associated with mood disorders such as early depression, anxiety, disease, violent behaviors, and personality disorders such as bipolar mental disorders, antisocial personality disorder, and schizophrenia. Social risk factors for drug use and addiction include male gender, being between 18 and 44, Native-American ancestry, unmarried marital status, and lower financial standing.

According to state statistics, people in the West are at a somewhat higher risk of chemical dependency. While men are more likely than women to develop a chemical dependency such as alcoholism, women tend to become more addicted to alcohol at much lower amounts.

•Adults exposed to negative settings as children are more prone to develop drug use disorders as adults.

Unpleasant experiences include not having parental supervision, seeing marital violence, having a parent who uses drugs, being physically abused, or being the victim of emotional or sexual abuse.

•What are the signs that you or someone you care about may be addicted to drugs?

While the exact symptoms used to diagnose drug use disorders are listed below, the following are warning signs that you or a loved one may be dealing with a drug problem:

•Mood issues such as impatience, melancholy, or mood swings

•Experiencing blackouts or memory loss

•Consistent family feuds

•Physical signs and symptoms of drug cessation

•Using drugs to cope with problems regularly

•Physical problems as a result of drug use

•Less time spent on life obligations as a result of drug use

- Taking more drugs to get high than usual

- Taking more prescriptions or for longer periods than advised

What are the symptoms and signs of drug addiction?

According to the DSM-5 (the Diagnostic and Statistical Manual of Mental Disorders, Fifth Edition), the diagnostic reference written and endorsed by the American Psychiatric Association, a person must exhibit a maladaptive pattern of drug use that leads to significant problems or stress, as manifested by at least two of the following symptoms.

- Recurrent drug use despite significant drug-related issues in the person's life (for example, in situations where the drug's effects could be physically harmful; recurrent legal problems as a result of drug use; repeated social or relationship problems as a result of or exacerbated by the drug's effects)

- Substance abuse prevents a person from doing important responsibilities at work, school, or home regularly.

- Legal difficulties arising from drug use regularly

- Tolerance is described as a drug's effect being drastically diminished or the need to dramatically increase the amount of the substance consumed to attain the same high or other desirable effects.

- Continued drug usage despite continuing or recurring social or romantic problems created or aggravated by the drug's effects

- Withdrawal is the psychological or physical signs or symptoms associated with the withdrawal from a specific substance or the use of that drug or a chemically similar medication to avoid withdrawal symptoms.

- A person spends an excessive amount of time getting, consuming, or recovering from the effects of the drug;

- The medicine is used in higher doses or for longer durations than recommended.

- The person has a strong urge to take the drug or has failed to minimize or manage their drug usage in the past.

- Cravings for the drug or a strong desire to use it.

- The person engages in negative decision-making by continuing to use the substance despite knowing that it is causing or exacerbating recurrent or recurring bodily or psychological issues;

• The person engages in significantly fewer or no vital social, work, recreational, or school activities due to substance abuse.

What happens to your brain when you use drugs?

While the effects of drugs on the brain vary depending on the drug, almost every drug misused affects the brain's working memory centers, as professionals refer to them.

Considering the activities of a chief executive in any organization will help you understand the functions of those areas: planning, organizing, prioritizing, and acting when it's time to act. Executive brain processes are often found in the frontal lobes of the brain, which comprise the frontal cortex and prefrontal cortex. When a person uses drugs, the inhibitory functions of the brain are severely compromised, causing the person to have difficulty resisting cravings that the brain would ordinarily delay or avoid. This loss of inhibition can lead to aggressive, sexual, criminal, dangerous, or other behaviors, all of which can have major consequences for the addict and those around him or her. Drug use during childhood or adolescence can negatively influence a person's ability to do all of these key executive tasks because the brain of persons under the age of 25 is still maturing and thus not completely matured.

What are the treatment alternatives for drug addiction?

The fact that most addicts underutilize drug addiction therapy is an unfortunate reality. According to data, less than 10% of persons with a milder substance-use disease seek professional help, while less than 40% of those with a more severe substance-use disorder do so. These data appear to be unrelated to socioeconomic or other demographic factors. They do, however, appear to be linked to the occurrence of other mental health problems (co-morbidity).

The main goals of drug-abuse treatment are abstinence, relapse prevention, and rehabilitation (also known as recovery). During the early stages of sobriety, a person suffering from chemical dependency may require support in preventing or lessening the effects of withdrawal. This procedure is known as detoxification or "detox." Medical specialists at a hospital or other inpatient institution often manage this component of drug addiction treatment. Drugs to help with withdrawal symptoms can be prescribed, as well as constant medical supervision. The medications used for detox are dictated by the substance to which the individual is addicted. Patients with alcohol use disorders may be given sedatives (benzodiazepines) or blood pressure medications to lower tremors and blood pressure or seizure medications to prevent seizures throughout the detoxification process.

For many substances of abuse, detox is the most difficult stage of dealing with the physical symptoms of addiction, and it usually lasts a few days to a few weeks.

Depending on the drug of addiction, physicians may utilize medicines to assist addicts in abstaining from drug use for a lengthy period. Addicts to opioids like Percodan (a mixture of aspirin and oxycodone hydrochloride), heroin, Vicodin, Vicodin ES, Anexsia, Lorcet Plus, Lorcet, or Norco (hydrocodone and acetaminophen), or Lorcet, Lorcet Plus, Vicodin, Vicodin ES, Anexsia, or Norco (combinations of hydrocodone and ascertain (Methadose). People addicted to alcohol may try to avoid drinking by using disulfiram (Antabuse), a drug that produces nausea, stomach cramps, and vomiting when ingested.

Recovery from the psychological aspects of drug addiction can be much more difficult and time-consuming than the physical parts. Outpatient treatment programs for less severe drug use disorders can address psychological addiction symptoms. Those with a more severe addiction, those who have relapsed after completing outpatient programs, and those who also have a severe mental health condition may benefit from the higher point of implementation, support, and monitoring provided in an inpatient drug and alcohol rehabilitation center, also known as "rehab." A sober living community, a

group-home setting where counselors provide daily sobriety support, structure, and monitoring, can aid many people with this type of drug use problem.

Drug addiction recovery requires self-help groups for

people with drug use disorders, such as Alcoholics Anonymous and Narcotics Anonymous, and organizations for addicts' loved ones, such as Al-Anon. Such groups, in particular, provide an emotionally safe atmosphere for people with substance use disorders and their loved ones to talk about their feelings and experiences and benefit from other people's experiences in their efforts to stay drug-free.

To treat drug addiction, it is also necessary to assist the addicted person's parents, other family members, and friends in refraining from supporting addictive behaviors (codependency). Preventing codependency among loved ones, whether through financial assistance, making excuses, or failing to address the drug abuser's drug desire and other maladaptive behaviors. Because minors are nearly always discovered in a family setting, emphasizing the addict's role becomes much more vital when the addict is a child or adolescent. Drug dependency treatment for children and adolescents differs from that for adults due to the impact of drugs on the developing brain, as well as the younger addict's tendency to require assistance completing their education and achieving higher education or job training compared to addicts who may have completed those aspects of their lives before developing the addiction.

When a person's mental illness is treated separately from his or her substance dependency, the treatment choices for dual diagnosis appear to be less effective.

Integrated treatment techniques that involve therapies for both illnesses are more effective. Assessment, intense case management, motivational treatments, behavior interventions, family treatment, and housing, rehabilitation, and medication management services are all included in such programs.

What are the consequences of drug addiction?

Addicts face potentially disastrous social, occupational, and medical consequences as a result of their addiction. Chemical dependency has several negative consequences for families, including an increased likelihood of domestic violence. Compared to persons who are not drug addicts, people with drug use disorders are substantially less likely to find and hold a job.

Children whose parents have a substance use disorder are more likely to have social, educational, and physical problems and be more likely to use drugs themselves.

In addition to the various severe social and occupational implications of drug addiction. A drug use issue can result in death, ranging from respiratory arrest due to heroin or sedative overdose to a heart attack or stroke caused by cocaine or amphetamine intoxication. People who are drug addicts are more likely to develop long-term medical issues. Drunkenness-related liver or heart failure and pancreatitis, as well as alcoholism or inhalant-related brain damage, are only a few examples.

What is the prognosis for drug addiction?

Treatment for alcoholism and other drug use problems improves the prognosis, but it is not without challenges. Periods of remission (no drug use) and relapse characterize recovery from substance addiction.

Is it possible to avoid drug addiction and abuse?

A variety of preventative strategies are useful in lowering the chance of developing a substance use problem. Increased physical exercise and other stress-reduction measures can help youth avoid developing a drug use disorder. More structured programs can also be beneficial. When the Raising Strong Children program, which involves teacher, parent, and student interventions, runs for 18 months or longer, it helps primary school children avoid drug addiction. The success of research-based prevention programs depends on tailoring them to the individual needs of children of various ages and the strengths and challenges of the community. Because of the widespread availability of technology, computer-based preventative methods have been developed. Regarding

how they compare to more traditional preventative initiatives and how many more people may be reached through technology, such programs are very promising.

ALTERATIONS IN THE BRAIN

Physical addiction appears to occur when long-term use of a drug changes how your brain experiences pleasure. The addictive substance causes physical changes in some nerve cells (neurons) in your brain. Neurotransmitters are chemicals that allow neurons to communicate with one another. After you stop using the drug, these changes can continue for a long period.

FACTORS THAT ARE AT RISK

Addiction affects people of all ages, genders, and socioeconomic backgrounds. A number of factors can influence the likelihood and speed with which an addiction develops:

•There is a family member who is addicted. Drug addiction runs in certain families and is most likely the result of a genetic predisposition. If you have a blood relative with an alcohol or drug addiction, such as a parent or sibling, you're more likely to develop a drug addiction.

•You have a mental health issue. If you have a mental health problem like depression, attention deficit hyperactivity disorder (ADHD), or post-traumatic stress disorder, you're more likely to become addicted to drugs. Drug use can become a coping method for uncomfortable emotions such as worry, despair, and loneliness, escalating the problem.

• Peer pressure exists. For young people, peer pressure is a major motivator to start using and abusing drugs.

• There is a lack of family participation. Addiction can be exacerbated by a lack of parental supervision, as well as unpleasant family situations or a lack of connection with your parents or siblings.

• Make the most of it right now. Early drug use can cause brain changes in children and increase the risk of developing a drug addiction.

· Using a chemical that is very addictive. Stimulants, cocaine, and opiate medicines, for example, may lead to addiction more quickly than others. Smoking or injecting drugs can make addiction worse. Taking so-called "light drugs," which are supposed to be less addictive, could put you on the road to addiction.

COMPLICATIONS

Short- and long-term impacts of drug usage can be considerable and harmful. Taking certain substances, especially in excessive dosages or in combination with other drugs or alcohol, can be extremely dangerous. Here are a few illustrations.

•Methamphetamine, opiates, and cocaine are highly addictive and can cause various short- and long-term health issues, including psychotic behavior, seizures, and overdose death.

•Side effects of GHB with flunitrazepam include sedation, confusion, and memory loss. These so-called "date rape pills" are known to impair one's ability to resist unwanted contact as well as recall the event. They can cause convulsions, coma, and death; the danger increases when these medicines are used with alcohol.

•Ecstasy (MDMA), commonly known as Molly (MDMA), can cause dehydration, electrolyte imbalance, and convulsions. MDMA has the potential to cause long- term brain damage.

•One of the most dangerous characteristics of club drugs is that the liquid, pill, or powder versions sold on the street usually contain unknown components, such as other illegally manufactured or pharmaceutical pharmaceuticals, which can be fatal.

- Inhalant users may suffer from varying degrees of brain damage due to the toxic nature of inhalants.

OTHER POTENTIALLY LIFE-ALTERING ISSUES

Addiction to drugs can lead to a variety of harmful and devastating consequences, including:

- Getting infected with a contagious disease. Through unsafe intercourse or sharing needles, addicts are more likely to get an infectious disease such as HIV.

- Other health concerns. Drug addiction can cause both short- and long-term mental and physical health problems. These are determined by the medication taken.

- Accidents. While under the influence of drugs, addicts are more likely to drive or participate in other risky actions.

- Suicide. People who are addicted to drugs are more prone than those who are not to commit suicide.

- Problems in the family. Changes in conduct can lead to marital or family problems, as well as challenges with custody.

- Concerns about the workplace Poor work performance,

absenteeism, and eventually job termination can result from drug misuse.

•School-related issues Drug abuse can harm academic performance and motivation.

•Legal issues. Drug users frequently face legal concerns such as purchasing or having illegal substances, stealing to fund their addiction, driving while under the influence of drugs or alcohol, and child custody disputes.

•There are financial difficulties. Spending money on drugs diverts income away from other needs, can lead to debt, and can lead to illegal or unethical behavior.

PREVENTION

The best way to avoid becoming addicted to a substance is to never use it in the first place. If your doctor recommends a medicine that has the potential to induce addiction, follow your doctor's recommendations carefully.

These medications should be provided in realistic amounts and quantities, and their use should be constantly monitored to ensure that they are not given too much or too long. Talk to your doctor if you think you need to take a drug in a larger dose than recommended.

PREVENTING CHILD AND ADOLESCENT DRUG ABUSE

Take the following steps to help your children and teenagers avoid drug abuse:

•Communicate. Talk to your kids about the consequences of drug use and misuse.

•Listen. Pay attention when your children discuss peer pressure and support them in their efforts to avoid it.

•Set a good example. Alcohol and other addictive substances should not be abused. Children whose parents abuse drugs are more prone to develop a drug addiction.

•Boost the bond's tensile strength. Attempt to strengthen your bond with your children. If you and your child have a strong, stable bond, your child's chances of taking or abusing drugs are minimized.

PREVENTING A RELAPSE

Once you've grown addicted to a substance, you're more likely to relapse into that behavior. Even if you've had treatment and haven't used the substance in a long period, resuming use is likely to result in you losing control.

•Follow your treatment plan to the letter. Keep an eye on your hunger levels. You might think you've recovered and that you don't need to do anything else to stay drug-free. Your chances of being drug-free will improve significantly if you

continue to see your therapist or counselor, attend support group meetings, and take prescription medication.

•Avoid high-risk situations at all costs. Don't go back to where you used to get your narcotics from a drug dealer. Also, avoid your drug-addicted friends.

•If you use the substance again, get help as soon as possible. If you begin to use the drug again, you should call your doctor, a mental health professional, or someone else who can help you right away.

Chapter 3: PSYCHEDELICS

Hallucinations. Vivid images. Sounds that are intense. Self-awareness is improved.

These are the trademark effects of the four most widely used psychedelic substances in the world. DMT, Ayahuasca, MDMA, and psilocybin mushrooms can all send users on a bizarre, mind-bending adventure that heightens their senses and strengthens their connection to the spirit world. However, not all trips are created equal; your high may only last a few hours if you drink ayahuasca. The rush from DMT, on the other hand, won't last more than 20 minutes.

Classic psychedelics are still potent, regardless of how long the high lasts. All four medicines have dramatic effects on neuronal activity, according to brain imaging studies. When you're drunk, your brain function is less constricted, which means you're more able to feel emotions. Furthermore, your brain's networks are significantly more connected, allowing for a higher level of consciousness and insight.

Because of these psychological benefits, researchers have argued that psychedelics could be beneficial therapeutic interventions. Many studies have revealed that these four drugs, in some form or another, can cure depression, anxiety, PTSD, addiction, and other mental health concerns. According to the theory, people who take psychedelics can open up their minds and address their painful pasts or self-destructive behavior without shame or fear. They are objective rather than emotionally detached.

These chemicals, however, are not without their drawbacks. However, recent research reveals that ayahuasca, DMT, MDMA, and psilocybin mushrooms can transform how doctors treat mental illness, particularly treatment-resistant patients. Although more research is needed to completely understand their impact on the human brain, what we do know so far is encouraging. Here's how each medicine affects your brain and how we might take advantage of it.

AYAHUASCA

Ayahuasca is a traditional plant-based beverage produced from the leaves of Psychotria Viridis and Banisteriopsis caapi vines. Amazonian Shamans have long used ayahuasca to alleviate illness and connect with the spiritual world. Certain religious organizations in Brazil consider the hallucinogenic drink to be a sacred sacrament. In recent years, ayahuasca has grown in popularity among ordinary people as a technique of enhancing self-awareness.

Because ayahuasca increases neuronal activity in the brain's visual cortex and limbic system - the memory and emotion-processing region deep inside the medial temporal lobe.

Dr. Jordi Riba, a leading ayahuasca researcher, explains, "Ayahuasca generates an introspective state of awareness during which people have highly personally important experiences." "It's typical to have emotionally charged, autobiographical memories appear in the mind's eye as visions, similar to those we have while sleeping."

According to Riba, ayahuasca consumers experience a "very strong" trip depending on the dose used. According to Riba, psychological effects occur after 45 minutes and peak after an hour or two; medically, the worst that a person can endure is nausea and vomiting. Unlike LSD or psilocybin mushrooms, those inebriated on ayahuasca are completely aware that they are hallucinating. Because of this self-conscious tripping, people have resorted to ayahuasca to help them overcome addiction and cope with traumatic situations. Riba and his team at Hospital do Sant Pau in Spain, Barcelona, have also begun "rigorous clinical trials" using ayahuasca to treat anxiety; so far, the plant-based drug was shown to reduce symptoms of depression in therapy patients, as well as produce "a very antibody response that is retained for weeks," according to Riba, who has studied this same drug with support from the National Institute of Mental Health.

His team is also looking at ayahuasca's post-acute effects, dubbed the "after-glow." So far, they've observed that during this "after-glow" phase, self-awareness-related brain regions have a greater link to other brain areas that control autobiographical memories and emotion. According to Riba, the mind is more open to psychosocial intervention at this time, so the research team is attempting to incorporate a small number of ayahuasca sessions into mindfulness psychotherapy.

"These functional modifications correlate with increased 'mindfulness' capacities," says Riba. "We believe that the combination of the ayahuasca experience and mindfulness training will increase the success rate of the psychotherapy intervention."

DMT

N, N-Dimethyltryptamine, and Ayahuasca are also known as DMT, have a close relationship. DMT is a compound found in the leaves of the Psychotria Viridis plant that causes hallucinations in ayahuasca users. DMT shares structural similarities with melatonin and serotonin, and it shares properties with psychedelics like magic mushrooms and LSD.

When taken orally, DMT has no impact on the body because stomach enzymes quickly break it down. In contrast, the Banisteriopsis caapi vines used in ayahuasca suppress those enzymes, allowing DMT to enter the bloodstream and travel to the brain. Like other classic psychedelics, DMT alters serotonin brain receptors, altering mood, perception, and a feeling of bodily integrity, according to the study. You're on a wild ride, to put it another way.

Much of what we know about DMT comes from Dr. Rick Strassman, who published the first substantial studies on the psychedelic drug two decades ago. DMT is one of the rare chemicals that can cross the blood-brain barrier. According to Strassman, this layer separates circulating blood from the extracellular fluid in the brain in the central nervous system. DMT's ability to cross these divides, according to Strassman, the author of two classic psychedelic books, implies that the molecule "appears to be a needed component of normal brain physiology."

"The brain only pulls things into its confines by using energy to get things past the blood-brain barrier for nutrients that it can't produce on its own — things like blood sugar or glucose," he continued. "DMT is unique in that it necessitates the brain's expenditure of energy for it to enter its confines."

DMT is a chemical that occurs naturally in the human body, particularly in the lungs. Strassman claims it can also be present in the pineal gland, a small region of the brain connected with the mind's "third eye." When combined with ayahuasca, the effects of highly potent DMT might last for hours. Strassman believes that when smoked or injected alone, the high lasts only a few minutes.

DMT's trip, according to Strassman, can be more powerful than other psychedelics, even if it's brief. DMT users have reported similar effects as ayahuasca users, including

a heightened feeling of self, more vivid images and sounds, and more time for reflection. Strassman has advised DMT in the past for depression, anxiety, and other mental health conditions and self-improvement and discovery. However, because of the lack of

studies on DMT, it's difficult to know the full scope of its therapeutic advantages.

Strassman adds, "There isn't a lot of research on DMT, and it has to be researched more."

MDMA

MDMA, unlike DMT, is not a naturally occurring hallucinogen. The chemical, often known as molly or ecstasy, is a synthetic concoction popular among ravers and club

kids. MDMA comes in the form of a capsule, tablet, or pill. The drug releases three important neurotransmitters: serotonin, dopamine, and norepinephrine (also known as ecstasy or molly). The synthetic drug also elevates oxytocin and prolactin levels, giving the user a feeling of euphoria and liberation. MDMA's most noteworthy side effect is the release of large serotonin levels, which depletes the brain's supply, resulting in days of depression after use.

According to brain imaging, MDMA causes a decrease in the amygdala – the almond- shaped portion of the brain that processes risks and fear – and an increase in activity in the prefrontal cortex, the brain's higher processing area. According to Dr. Michael Mithoefer, who has done extensive research on MDMA and its effects on various neural networks, ongoing research on psychedelics and their impact on various neural network models has uncovered that MDMA allows for further flexibility in brain activity, which means that people tripping on the drug can filter emotions and feelings without being "stuck in old ways of processing."

"People are less likely to be overwhelmed by concern and are better suited to digest experience without becoming numb to emotion," he claims.

Last year, the US Food and Drug Administration permitted researchers to move forward with preparations for a large-scale clinical trial to look into the effects of MDMA as a treatment for post-traumatic stress disorder (PTSD). Mithoefer oversaw phase-two trials supported by the Multidisciplinary Association for Psychedelic Studies (MAPS), an American nonprofit founded in the mid-1980s that influenced the FDA's decision. People with PTSD could face their trauma without withdrawing from their emotions while under the effect of MDMA during the study because of the intricate link between the amygdala and the prefrontal cortex. Based on the excellent outcomes of the phase two studies, Mithoefer told Rolling Stone in December that he expected the FDA to approve the phase three trial plans early this year.

Despite the positive results of investigations exploring MDMA's use for PTSD treatment, Mithoefer cautions that the drug should not be used outside of a therapeutic environment because it causes nausea, muscle tension, increased appetite, sweating, chills and blurred vision. MDMA can cause dehydration, kidney failure, heart failure, and an erratic pulse, among other things. If the user does not drink enough water or has an underlying health concern, MDMA's side effects can be lethal.

PSILOCYBIN MUSHROOMS

Mushrooms are another hallucinogenic with a long history of use in health and healing rituals, particularly in Asia. People tripping on mushrooms will experience intense hallucinations within an hour of intake due to the body's breakdown of psilocybin, a found naturally psychedelic component found in more than 200 types of mushrooms.

According to Imperial College London research published in 2014, psilocybin, a serotonin receptor, increases connectivity between parts of the brain that are normally separated. Scientists compared fMRI brain scans of people who took psilocybin to people who took a placebo and discovered that magic mushrooms generate a distinct brain connection pattern that is only present while people are hallucinating. The brain acts with less constraint and more intercommunication in this state; according to Imperial College London researchers, this type of psilocybin-induced brain activity is related to dreaming and heightened emotional well-being.

"These stronger connections are responsible for developing a new state of consciousness," says Dr. Paul Expert, a methodologist and physicist who took part in the Imperial College London study. "Psychedelics have the potential to be a really powerful tool for learning more about normal brain function."

According to new research, magic mushrooms may be effective in treating depression and other mental health conditions. According to Expert, psilocybin, like ayahuasca, can block activity in the default mode network of the brain, and individuals who have tripped on mushrooms have experienced feeling "a heightened degree of euphoria and closeness to the world." A high dose of mushrooms alleviated depressed symptoms in treatment-resistant individuals, according to research published in the British medical journal The Lancet last year.

According to the same study, psilocybin can treat anxiety, addiction, and obsessive- compulsive disorder due to its mood-elevating properties. Other research has found that psilocybin can reduce the fear response in rats, implying that the drug could treat PTSD.

Despite these promising results, psychedelic research is restricted, and eating magic mushrooms is extremely dangerous. According to Expert, psilocybin users may suffer paranoia or ego disintegration, the complete loss of subjective self-identity. Their physical and psychological settings will have an impact on how they react to the hallucinogenic drug. Expert urges caution when using magic mushrooms because the good or negative effects on the person could be "deep (and uncontrollable) and long-lasting." "We can't properly manage the psychedelic experience because we don't fully know the process underpinning psychedelics' cognitive effects."

WHAT HAPPENS TO YOUR BRAIN WHEN YOU TAKE AYAHUASCA'S HALLUCINOGENIC?

As clinicians and academics realize that psychedelics can assist with depression, anxiety, and PTSD, understanding how they affect the brain is becoming increasingly crucial.

While some psychedelics, such as ketamine and LSD, have been thoroughly examined, researchers are increasingly turning their attention to lesser-known psychedelics, such as ayahuasca, a strong brew associated with the Amazon rainforest peoples and tribes.

DMT (N, N-dimethyltryptamine), a fast-acting psychedelic known to create intense visual hallucinations in a group of healthy people, is a component of ayahuasca.

DMT is one of the main psychoactive ingredients in

ayahuasca, a psychedelic beverage. Boiling leaves from the Psychotria Viridis shrub and stalks from the Banisteriopsis caapi vine are used to make it.

Researchers are now trying to figure out how this medicine impacts the brain. Researchers in the United Kingdom monitored the brain's electrical activity to better understand the effects of DMT in a recent study.

Their findings shed new light on the drug's impact on brain function and consciousness, as well as its therapeutic potential.

What the research discovered

The effects of intravenous DMT were studied in this study, which was published in the journal Scientific ReportsTrusted Source.

According to the study's authors at Imperial College London's Centre for Psychedelic Research, brain activity suggests that DMT-induced images are comparable to those experienced while dreaming.

"It's apparent these people are thoroughly engrossed in their experience based on the altered brain waves and participant testimonies. It's similar to daydreaming but much more vivid and immersive. Lead author Christopher Timmermann, a Ph.D. candidate in neuropsychopharmacology at Imperial College London, described it as "like dreaming but with your eyes open."

Ayahuasca is usually used for religious and spiritual purposes, with participants being guided through a strong hallucinogenic experience by a shaman or curandero.

However, in recent years, ayahuasca's appeal has spread beyond its geographical and cultural confines.

The scientific community has become more interested in it and other psychedelic chemicals such as psilocybin mushrooms and MDMA for various potential therapeutic effects.

Although the study published this week does not explicitly address ayahuasca, it does show how DMT impacts the brain.

"It's an intriguing, well-conducted study because it supports the idea that the pattern of brain activity during a psychedelic experience is comparable to that observed during sleep in many ways. Draulio Araujo, Ph.D., a professor of neurology at the Federal University of Rio Grande do Norte (UFRN) in Natal, Brazil, who has extensively investigated the effects of ayahuasca, believes that the nature of the visions typically associated with psychedelics is closer to dreams than hallucinations.

Araujo was not involved in the study.

Timmermann and his colleagues enlisted the help of 13 healthy volunteers to test an intravenous medication solution against a placebo. Before, during, and after the infusion, all were provided with caps with electrodes to record EEG electrical activity.

DMT caused a dip in alpha waves, the major electrical wave in people when they are awake, and a transient increase in theta waves, which indicate dreaming compared to placebo.

"Brain waves have varied frequencies in the normal brain, some slower than others, and these frequency ranges are given names... Dr. Derek Chong, vice chair of neurology and director of epilepsy at Lenox Hill

Hospital in New York City, explained that these rhythms fluctuate depending on whether we are awake, tired, or in various stages of sleep.

"We typically see the slower frequencies take over during drowsiness, especially when medicines are administered to cause sleepiness. They saw some of that in this study.

Still, they also saw rhythmicity (oscillatory power), which I believe the authors are claiming implies alterations or possibly release of new brain activity, not just sleepiness," Chong explained.

Overall, brain activity was more chaotic and distinct from other psychedelics like psilocybin or LSD.

PSYCHEDELICS AS MEDICINE

The findings could also offer light on DMT's potential as an antidepressant, a field into which other researchers have already ventured.

Prior study has shown that DMT (ingested via ayahuasca) has fast-acting antidepressant benefits in those with depression, even though the evidence is limited.

Psilocybin mushrooms, another classic psychedelic, are also being investigated as a potential treatment for depression in the United States and internationally.

Still, additional research on DMT and ayahuasca is needed before determining whether they may be used to treat depression or other ailments.

"What I believe the study will accomplish is give DMT a scientifically validated status, making it more acceptable for future recommended use for psychiatric or psychological purposes," Chong added.

EARLY PSYCHEDELIC RESEARCH

The success of these psilocybin trials indicates that psychedelic research is reviving, although there are still numerous obstacles to overcome.

This is partly due to societal perceptions about these drugs, which have altered since Wasson's early research with psilocybin in the 1950s.

Psychedelics like psilocybin and LSD gained popularity during the 1960s hippie and counterculture movements due to the intense nature of the experiences they created.

It also sparked a flurry of research into how these medications functioned and whether they provided therapeutic benefits.

More than 1,000 publications on LSD, another psychedelic, had been published by 1961. This includes studies on LSD and psilocybin by Harvard psychologists Timothy Leary, Ph.D., and Richard Alpert, Ph.D. (later known as Ram Dass).

The lack of public worry about drugs at the time aided this early cultural and scientific blooming, which may seem odd considering our present concentration on illegal drugs.

In 1960, people were not as concerned about drugs as they are now. So you weren't hitting up against any taboos if you wanted to do some creative, think-out-of-the-box experimentation.

The media and cultural craze surrounding psychedelics, on the other hand, would soon come to an end, presumably due to the substances' extreme popularity.

There were concerns and fears about these drugs being

used in a much more liberal context — such as people taking it wherever and not knowing what they're taking, and all of these things with black market acid and counterculture use of acid

In the early 1970s, some countries classified psilocybin and other psychedelics as Schedule 1 narcotics, which are substances with a high potential for abuse and no medical purpose, according to the government.

As a result, these substances' recreational use has transferred to the illegal market. And research into these medicines' potential medicinal applications was virtually halted.

Drug classification does not preclude study on them or their usage for medical purposes. It's also not irrational for academics to look into their potential benefits.

"I have no difficulty with the idea that something can be fully restricted for recreational use — and even subject to severe sanctions if it has a recognized medical use," Caulkins said.

Cocaine and methamphetamine, in reality, are both Schedule 2 substances with limited medicinal applications.

Medical marijuana's popularity as a treatment for pain, HIV, addiction, and other ailments suggests progress in reopening prohibited drugs for research.

"The federal government does support research, specifically on cannabis, to attempt to grasp its potential," Caulkins said.

LONG-TERM STIGMA

Despite this, the stigma associated with psychedelics persists today. Researchers dispute the reasons behind this.

We were coming off a decade in which many American cities appeared to be breaking apart with tremendous amounts of street violence connected with crack cocaine.

This may have influenced popular perceptions of other illegal drugs, such as marijuana and psychedelics, even if these drugs resulted in fewer deaths than the thousands of people killed each year by prescription opioids.

According to Garcia-Romeu, the current political context resembles that of the 1960s, when the pushback against psychedelics began, with a huge left-leaning counterculture set against a conservative backdrop.

"There's certainly a strong conservative base — in politics, in particular — that regards drugs like cannabis or hallucinogens like psilocybin or LSD as drugs of abuse," he said.

However, there are hints that these attitudes are changing and increasing openness to these medications.

Are psychedelics becoming more mainstream?

Is this to say that psychedelic research has entered the mainstream?

"I don't think we would say they're quite mainstream at this point," Garcia-Romeu said, "but I do believe they have a chance to become mainstream in the next 10 or 20 years." "If we can continue to do meticulous research and avoid any major setbacks."

The stigma attached to these medications, on the other hand, continues to hinder efforts to raise funds for new research.

"Despite the research's potential thus far, legislators, federal agencies, and major scientific grant funding agencies are still reticent to financially support it. According to Brad Burge, director of communications and marketing at the nonprofit Multidisciplinary Association for Psychedelic Studies (MAPS), that's due to the substances' long-standing stigma.

Even if they have financing, strict federal oversight and the Schedule 1 designation make it difficult for researchers to investigate these medications. Medicine can only be lifted off Schedule 1 if sufficient study demonstrates a medicinal advantage to complicate matters.

Some believe that "this has created a bit of a paradox" because "you can't establish value [of a drug] because you can't truly research the drug, and so you can't demonstrate that it has value," according to Dyck.

Despite these obstacles, some research continues to progress.

MAPS collaborate with the FDA to complete phase III clinical studies of MDMA- assisted psychotherapy for

PTSD (PTSD).

MDMA, commonly known as 3,4-methylenedioxymethamphetamine, is a stimulant that also has hallucinogenic properties. This molecule is present in ecstasy and molly,

though these drugs may be contaminated with other substances or not contain any MDMA at all when sold on the street.

MAPS is a treatment that uses pure MDMA to reduce PTSD symptoms and maintain them down indefinitely, without the need for further treatment.

People with PTSD will take pure MDMA two or three times in the phase III experiment, along with 12 weeks of psychotherapy.

"These are people who have PTSD that is chronic and resistant to treatment," Burge explained. "They've been suffering from PTSD for a long time. They've tried other medicines, and none of them have worked."

Military veterans and sexual assault victims with PTSD were included in earlier smaller studies, with results promising enough to continue forward with phase III trials through the Food and Drug Administration (FDA).

"We discovered that two-thirds of individuals no longer qualified for PTSD after a single 12-week session of MDMA-assisted psychotherapy, during which participants ingested MDMA on two occasions separated by four weeks," said Burge.

Only 103 persons took part in these early MDMA trials in people with PTSD. However, multiple clinical research involving over 1,200 volunteers found no evidence of long- term MDMA usage or cognitive impairment.

MAPS anticipates receiving formal FDA permission in February and beginning the study in June.

"If we achieve findings that are remotely comparable to the outcomes that we observed in phase II, and assuming that we acquire the funds that we need to complete those trials," Burge added, "We anticipate to get approval in the coming years."

The phase III experiment will cost between $25 and $30 million in total. MAPS has raised $10 million to date, entirely from tiny foundations and hundreds of private individuals. Burge believes it is "reasonable" to raise the additional monies over three to four years.

This is a minor price to pay compared to the billions of dollars that pharmaceutical companies spend on research and development each year, especially for a treatment that will have a long-term impact.

"Unlike traditional medications, which individuals often take every day for years or decades just to regulate their symptoms," Burge explained, "we're creating a treatment

now that may be able to drastically diminish those symptoms overtime after just a few treatments."

Taking care of serious issues

Even with MAPS and other groups of researchers' triumphs, moving forward with a study into the therapeutic benefits of psychedelics will necessitate addressing two main concerns: the potential of abuse and the possibility of drugs ending up wherever they aren't supposed to be.

Both of these issues can be mitigated by the way psychedelic drug treatment programs are set up.

"If the suggestion is, 'I want a doctor at a hospital to be able to provide a single dose of LSD in a controlled setting,' the risk of increased LSD use by 17-year-old teenagers is virtually zero," Caulkins explained.

MAPS envisions MDMA-assisted psychotherapy for PTSD working in this way, according to Burge. The medication would be given out in a dedicated clinic staffed by doctors, nurses, and mental health specialists.

People would have the medicine administered on-site and stay overnight or longer, reducing the chance of the substance being given — or sold — to someone else.

The minimal number of dosages given to patients throughout their treatment would also reduce the likelihood of abuse.

"The risk for misuse with pure MDMA, given a restricted number of times — two or three times in a clinical situation — does not appear to be very worrying at all," Burge said.

Psychedelics' mystical effects have not been forgotten,

despite the development of practical treatments for illnesses such as anxiety, depression, and addiction.

Researchers at Johns Hopkins University initiate a new study to see if psilocybin might help religious leaders develop their spiritual lives.

This form of inquiry could complement Western science, which tends to avoid important issues like spirituality.

"It's tough to ask these large abstract, philosophical, or spiritual questions," Dyck explained, "but there may be a growing hunger for bringing scientific methodologies back to ask these kinds of more humanist questions."

Lower Risk of Mental Illness Linked to Psychedelic Drugs

New research debunks decades of beliefs, claiming that psychedelics are not linked to mental illness and may have beneficial long-term impacts on users.

"Wouldn't you like to see a positive LSD story on the news?" comedian Bill Hicks famously said. To make your selection based on facts rather than fear and superstition? Perhaps? That would be fascinating, wouldn't it? For a single time?"

This is that story.

There is no link between psychedelic drugs like LSD, mushrooms, mescaline, or peyote and a variety of mental health concerns, according to a study published in the journal PLOS One. Mental health difficulties such as psychosis, mood disorders, anxiety disorders, and general psychological suffering are associated with psychedelic use.

In a press release, researcher Teri Krebs stated, "Many people describe extremely significant experiences and lasting good impacts from consuming psychedelics."

THE SOCIETAL EFFECTS OF PSYCHEDELICS

The Department of Neuroscience at the Norwegian University of Science and Technology analyzed data from more than 130,000 Americans who participated in the National Survey on Drug Use and Health. They discovered that taking psychedelic drugs does not cause mental disease but instead may help to prevent it.

Major psychological distress, outpatient mental health therapy, and psychiatric medicine prescriptions were lower in people who used psilocybin or mescaline throughout their lives and those who used LSD in the previous year.

"Other examinations have shown no evidence of healthcare and social problems amongst people who have used psychedelic drugs hundreds of times in legally protected religious rites," clinical psychologist Pl-rjan Johansen said.

While some people may have bad experiences with these drugs, experts argue that psychedelic drugs do not live up to their reputation on a societal level. According to studies, almost two million people in the United States have used LSD, psilocybin, or mescaline at some point in their lives.

"Early speculation that psychedelics could induce mental health issues was based on a small number of case reports and did not consider either the widespread use of psychedelics or the common occurrence of mental health problems in the general

population" Krebs continued. "Psychedelics have been

used by tens of millions of people over the last 50 years, with little indication of long-term harm."

A Psychedelic Users' Safe Haven

It's no surprise that psychedelic drug experimentation is popular at large music events like Coachella and Burning Man. The noise and crowd, on the other hand, can be overwhelming for intoxicated people.

At this year's Burning Man festival, Burners will be able to relax and receive "psychedelic harm reduction services" from volunteers from the Multidisciplinary Association for Psychedelic Studies (MAPS). Last year, according to the organization, AlterNet aided 108 festival-goers who were under the influence of psychedelics, none of whom required medical attention or incarceration.

Cameron Bowman, a.k.a. The Festival Lawyer, advised festival-goers to use psychedelics on legal matters. He recommends remaining discrete, being aware of undercover cops, and exercising your right to silence.

If a cop stops you, Bowman suggests asking, "Am I being detained?" right away. Why? Is it safe for me to leave now, or am I being held?"

Chapter 4: DIMETHYLTYPTAMINE (DMT)

DMT is a hallucinogen that is similar to LSD and magic mushrooms in terms of its effects. We dig deeper into what it is and how it works.

N-dimethyltryptamine (DMT) is a psychedelic tryptamine found in a wide range of plants and animals. It's also known as fantasia or the spirit molecule because of the profound hallucinogenic experience it provides.

DMT is a white crystalline powder obtained from various plants found worldwide, but particularly in South America. It can also be created in a laboratory. It's usually smoked or vaporized in a pipe or ingested orally in ayahuasca brews.

WHAT ARE DMT'S SIDE EFFECTS?

DMT has a strong psychological effect, causing acute visual and aural hallucinations, euphoria, and a distorted perception of space, body, and time. It's been described as intense, similar to a near-death experience, and it can be overwhelming or scary.

DMT's effects are determined by various elements, including the amount consumed, age, mood, personality, and ambient influences. The following are some examples of generic effects:

- Increased blood pressure
- Increased heart rate
- Chest pains or tightness
- Dilated pupils
- Agitation
- Dizziness
- Rapid rhythmic eye movements
- Nausea, vomiting

Some people report feeling uncomfortable or agitated for weeks after using DMT, according to reports. Some folks say they're having trouble integrating the trip into their daily lives and maintaining their sense of self.

WHAT ARE THE DMT RISKS?

Serotonin, the brain neurotransmitter responsible for sensations of well-being and happiness, is structurally connected to DMT. This means there's a higher chance of developing serotonin syndrome, a potentially fatal disorder caused by the body's

overproduction of serotonin. If you're already using anti-depressants, you're at a higher risk. Agitation, confusion, a very high temperature, and perhaps coma and death are some symptoms.

The physical side effects of DMT, which include an increase in heart rate and blood pressure, might be dangerous, especially if you already have heart disease or high blood pressure. Seizures, a loss of muscle coordination that raises the risk of falling and injury, respiratory distress, and confusion are other dangers.

Long-term psychological consequences, such as chronic psychosis and Hallucinogen Persisting Perception Disorders, may occur, like with other hallucinogenic substances (HPPD). These diseases are uncommon and can affect anyone, while research shows that persons with a history of psychological difficulties are more likely to experience them.

While no medicine is completely risk-free, several precautions can be taken to lessen the dangers.

•Lower dosages are usually safer.

•Avoid combining alcohol with other medications because the combined effects might be unpredictable and increase the danger, especially with antidepressants.

•As with any drug usage, it's ideal to have people around you who you can trust and who know how to administer first aid, as with any drug use.

A DMT trip is compared as "breaking out of a simulation" by users. People claim to be able to access the true inner workings of their minds and describe feeling propelled into other realms, where their consciousness resides outside of their bodies.

Another user called Eli* told Business Insider, "One may sense coalescence with the very fabric of space-time, followed by the 'blast-off' into another, alien dimension, referred to by some as 'hyperspace.'" "The parallel reality defies all predictions, manifesting as incomprehensible geometric fractal shapes that have a striking likeness to our own."

Although time and language are incomprehensible, he claims you may conduct telepathic conversations with the beings you meet. A DMT trip varies from hallucinating on other drugs like psilocybin (mushrooms) or LSD in that it takes you to another world rather than changing your relationship with it, according to personal accounts.

Some users have trouble explaining the experience because it is so vivid and abstract. According to one user, attempting to write it down is essentially useless. However, DMT users frequently state that it makes them feel "more real than real."

Many of the users I met with recounted their brains being "torn" from their bodies and led through a vivid, circus-like landscape by alien aliens or spiritual beings. Even specialized characters who frequently feature, such as a jester, have their boards.

DMT RESEARCH BEGAN IN THE 1950S.

In the 1950s, a Hungarian scientist named Stephen Szára discovered that DMT was psychedelic. In the 1960s, it was discovered in the human body, with research revealing that it is generated in the lungs and brain pineal gland. It's thought to be present in the natural world, in thousands of plants, and in every mammal that has been researched so far.

There was a frenzy of DMT research in the 1960s, including if it could help explain why some people developed schizophrenia (it couldn't). However, DMT was classed as a prohibited substance in the 1970s, and the study was halted.

Between 1990 and 1995, Rick Strassman, a psychologist, and psychopharmacologist, and his colleague Clifford Qualls undertook the first new human research into DMT in a generation in the United States.

"I was attracted to looking into DMT as a naturally present hallucinogenic for quite a few reasons," he told Business Insider. "One of them was enthralled with the biology of naturally occurring spiritual states. Certain signs and symptoms of a near-death experience, religious, a mystical enlightenment experience. It's also likely that naturally occurring DMT contributed to such non-drug experiences."

Many spiritual and religious societies use breathing exercises to help them achieve enlightenment. If DMT is created in the lungs, it may explain how people get "psychedelic" trance states while meditating.

Strassman enlisted the help of seasoned psychedelic users for the DMT study. He advised them to take DMT in a therapeutic context and report back after the hallucinations were gone. With a standard dose, the effects of a DMT trip usually last 30 to 40 minutes.

"There were no bells, sirens, or Buddhist statues – just 'here's the prescription, and tell me what happened when you come down.'" Strassman claims that. "It was like sending

someone off to explore a new nation and then expecting them to come back with a report on what they discovered."

Because DMT breaks down too quickly in the stomach to provide psychedelic effects if swallowed, it is normally smoked or injected.

People regularly report profound experiences after coming down from a DMT high, such as remembering their background. Some people saw abstract images that told them they needed to spend more time with their families. According to Strassman, one of the ladies in the study returned convinced that consciousness can survive death.

"One of the participants had a textbook near-death experience," he explained, "which confirmed her beliefs and made her feel good about dying." "She stated, 'If everyone knew what was waiting for them after death, everyone would commit suicide,' to which I responded, 'Well, don't spread the information.'"

DMT is closely linked to spiritualism and death.

For a long time, there has been a link between DMT and spiritualism. According to one theory, DMT is assumed to be in the body because we release a large amount of it when we die. Some people believe that seeing a white light or divine entities after a near- death experience is due to a release of DMT, which gives the brain one last, all- encompassing hallucination.

Ayahuasca is a combination of DMT and a plant containing an enzyme inhibitor that prevents DMT from breaking down in the Amazon. A DMT beverage has been enjoyed for over 500 years as a result of this process.

"

According to Strassman, ayahuasca is a Quechua phrase that means "death vine" or "soul vine." "As a result, some individuals believe that consuming ayahuasca will allow them to enter the world of the dead or disembodied spirits." This has been a prevalent notion around ayahuasca, or DMT, for a long time."

To check if DMT is present in near-death experiences, researchers could utilize a variety of approaches. You may, for example, invite someone who's had a near-death experience to try DMT and compare the results. Strassman said he'd had a few emails from people who were describing a lot of similarities.

You can also test DMT levels in someone who has had a near-death experience or look at the expression of the gene responsible for DMT synthesis in dying patients.

The unpublished study suggests that DMT levels rise in the brains of dying animals, according to Strassman. He feels that by conducting additional research in this area, the link can be strengthened.

DMT may be able to provide solutions to some brain-related questions.

According to Strassman, DMT research could help us discover certain components of consciousness in the future.

He explained, "I'm a huge fan of Aristotle's classic account of the mind, with its intellectual and creative activities." "I believe that psychedelics in general, and DMT in particular, must stimulate the imaginative rather than the rational capacities of the mind... DMT may be able to help us understand how the imaginative faculty functions if we start looking only at biology or neurophysiology of the creative faculty vs. the logical faculty."

Many questions remain unanswered, like what DMT

does in the body in the first place. According to Strassman, it's significant since energy is used to convey it into the brain actively. Only a few chemicals, such as glucose and amino acids, are absorbed by the brain and are required for proper brain function but are not created by the body.

"It makes you wonder if DMT is also involved in typical everyday consciousness modulation," Strassman said. "In recent years, it has also been discovered that the enzyme and gene responsible for DMT production are quite active in the retina. As a result, DMT could influence visual perception as well as consciousness management."

I'll leave it to you to figure out what this implies regarding the idea that we're living in a simulation.

DMT is rapidly destroyed in the human body, which makes it difficult to analyze. As a result, a trip only takes around half an hour. In 2016, Strassman and his colleague Andrew Gallimore published a paper that detailed a way for continually injecting DMT over some time.

There are two benefits to this: one, the effect can be characterized more precisely, and two, it has the potential to produce therapeutic results.

"A lot of individuals talk about the therapeutic benefits of ayahuasca," Strassman added, "and you could use it for therapeutic purposes if you could extend the DMT state." "It would be more realistic to prolong the condition and determine if it has therapeutic consequences," says the researcher.

DMT has a profound effect on humans, regardless of how it is consumed.

DMT users believe the drug has a lot of potentials, both in terms of opening people's minds and being used to treat mental illnesses.

According to Sam, the hallucinogenic can "raise global human consciousness and revolutionize the current age."

He claimed that he was suffering from an existential crisis and was suicidal at times since he couldn't understand the significance of anything before ingesting DMT.

"I got to the point where I was so sick of living that I determined to commit suicide unless I could be given a decent cause to live," he explained. "I knew I wanted to make a difference in the world," says the young woman.

In some ways, however, it seemed pointless to even try. "It was as though the cosmos wrapped me in a comfortable ocean of love when DMT gave me the answer."

After then, he maintains, his cynicism was replaced with hope. He felt re-energized and revitalized as if he could start his life over with a "new optimistic and clear perspective."

In addition to the awareness that users of hallucinogenics often talk about, Sam believed DMT genuinely dragged him back from the edge. He'd gotten the answers he was looking for, but he'd also gained a new perspective on life.

"Before agreeing to the suicide plot, I reasoned to myself that I should try DMT as a last resort." Thankfully, the outcome was better than I could have hoped for, and I can honestly say that it saved my life," he said. "I believe DMT has the potential to be a revolutionary drug in the therapeutic setting... As the planet transforms, I feel we are nearing a new phase of human civilization."

Anthony Castellanos regards himself as one of the most experienced DMT users. Medicine can be used to treat anxiety, stress, and depression, according to Business Insider. He believed he got access to his imagination's "deep sections" for four months after one trip.

"With simple meditation, I could drift away into other locations far from my body," he claimed. "I had a portal within me through which my spirit could visit the realms of love, beauty, and God," she says. "I'm not even a religious person."

Some people are also pessimistic.

DMT, like any other drug, should be used with prudence, according to Castellanos.

"It has the potential to be mentally harmful because of its vivid endless intensity," he stated. "It takes one out of his or her normal perspective of reality, and some people find it difficult to adjust following a journey."

DMT research is just getting started, according to Strassman. Unfortunately, other scientists are inclined to dismiss it as a research topic, believing that DMT concentrations in the human brain are too low to be meaningful.

"It's very bad those ideas are being pushed," he continued, "because they are impeding research into this incredibly important topic." "And that's a little strange... Even if overall brain concentrations are modest, this does not rule out the possibility of large concentrations in specific brain locations.

"In many ways, the brain is a giant enigmatic black box, but we're learning more and more about it."

There are risks associated with all drugs, and some people believe that this is a barrier to openly using recreational drugs. According to Talk to Frank, a drug awareness and advice website, a bad trip on any drug, including DMT, can cause mental health problems or worsen existing ones. It can also raise blood pressure and heart rate, dangerous for people with heart disease.

Regardless, DMT has a sizable following, both among people who use it and those who want to try it. Many supporters of recreational drug use argue that legalizing drugs and regulating drugs like DMT would make them safer to use while also enhancing the benefits.

Researchers may have only recently begun to explore DMT's possibilities, regardless of where it originated. And, wherever the investigation takes place, there will almost certainly be a large number of people following the story as the riddles unfold.

"DMT is an antidote for existential dread," Eli explained. "It illustrates how meaningless and ephemeral our physical existence is, and it is through this realization that one may realize and appreciate how remarkable it is to be alive."

SHORT-TERM EFFECTS OF DMT

People seeking a psychedelic "trip" similar to that generated by LSD or psilocybin frequently utilize DMT. Many drug users over LSD prefer DMT because the trip is much shorter, lasting just 30 to 45 minutes rather than several hours as with LSD.

The medicine has a quick onset, and the effects are usually felt right away.

A common effect of a psychedelic DMT trip is 1,2,3:

- Time and space perceptions are altered.
- Having an out-of-body experience.
- Hallucinations, both visual and auditory
- Extremely happy feelings.
- Perceived epiphanies or insights (often believed to have come from aliens, divinities, or other mystical beings).
- The color perception is brighter and more intense.

SIDE EFFECTS

DMT's physiological side effects include 1,2:

- A faster heart rate.
- Rapid eye movement is unintentional.
- Hypertension (high blood pressure).
- Pupils that are dilated.
- Issues with coordination.

- Vomiting and nausea (typically when taken in oral forms such as ayahuasca).

- Dizziness.

- Respiratory arrest and/or coma (reported in high doses).

BAD TRIPS

While the DMT journey is psychologically rewarding for some people, others may have a "bad trip."

The following 2,3 things could happen on a bad trip:

- Perplexity or disorientation

- A sense of powerlessness

- Fear, worry, grief, rage, or agitation are all negative emotions.

- Images or sounds that are violent or unpleasant.

- Anxiety about going nuts.

- The fear of dying.

- Reliving traumatic memories or experiences.

EFFECTS OF DMT ABUSE IN THE LONG TERM

To assess the long-term detrimental effects of DMT

intake, more research is needed. According to the study, DMT does not appear to cause tolerance in users.

Long-term DMT use is the most dangerous psychologically, as it puts the user at risk of developing psychosis and experiencing continuous flashbacks and hallucinations.

Flashbacks can occur without notice and at any time. Months or even years later, some users may experience flashbacks to their drug usage. Visual or aural hallucinations, as well as terrible emotions or experiences, may resurface during flashbacks, making you feel as though you're reliving your hallucinogenic trip.

The use of traditional hallucinogens, such as DMT, regularly can lead to persistent psychosis. Some of the indications and symptoms of persistent psychosis include:

- Irrational thinking
- Anxiety and irritability.
- Disturbances in vision

- The paranoia persists.

Another mental health concern that might arise from using hallucinogens frequently is hallucinogen persistent perception disorder (HPPD). Some of the signs and symptoms are as follows:

- Hallucinations, both visual and auditory

- Symptoms are comparable to other neurological disorders such as brain tumors and cerebrovascular accidents (i.e., stroke).

ADDICTION TO DMT

While DMT does not induce physical dependence, some people may abuse it to the point where they experience various problems. This is especially true in polysubstance abuse, where the user mixes DMT with additional psychoactive drugs. "Other hallucinogen use disorder" describes a pattern of problematic hallucinogen use that causes significant problems or pain. Some of the signs and symptoms are as follows:

- Attempting unsuccessfully to control or stop DMT use.

- Ingesting more DMT than is recommended.

- Investing a significant amount of time and effort in getting and utilizing DMT and recuperating from its effects.

- Ignoring personal responsibilities in favor of DMT use.

- You have a strong desire for DMT.

- Giving up previously enjoyed habits or pastimes to utilize DMT

- Using DMT despite increasing negative interpersonal, social, or physical/mental health consequences.

TREATMENT FOR DMT ADDICTION

Currently, there are no FDA-approved medications to treat DMT addiction. Those addicted to DMT can seek effective behavioral treatment to help them reduce their drug use and recover. Some examples of behavioral therapy and treatment that may be beneficial to someone struggling with DMT abuse are as follows:

- Individual or group therapy: Individual or group therapy to address the root reasons of abuse.

- Cognitive-behavioral therapy (CBT): A type of therapy

that teaches patients how to regulate desires healthily and avoid relapse.

• 12-step programs: Support groups that provide a step-by-step approach to recovery while surrounded by people who have faced similar addictions and struggles.

• Contingency management (behavioral incentives): A approach that uses prizes and other forms of positive reinforcement to reward and reinforce specified desired behaviors, such as abstinence.

• Motivational interviewing: A type of counseling that assists the client in understanding his or her internal motivation, resulting in behavioral change.

• Inpatient rehabilitation: for a period of 30 to 90 days, addiction therapy is administered 24 hours a day, seven days a week. A combination of the therapeutic methods outlined above will likely be used in this type of therapy program.

DMT STAYS IN YOUR SYSTEM FOR HOW LONG?

DMT affects the brain's serotonin and other neurotransmitter receptors. It can cause agitation, anxiety, or terror in certain people.

- A distorted perception of one's own body
- Euphoria
- Difficulties concentrating, making judgments, or recalling information
- Vivid visual hallucinations
- Nausea or vomiting

It can also induce physical changes in the following areas:

- Blood pressure levels
- The temperature of the body
- Pulse rate
- Respiration

People with schizophrenia and other mental health disorders should avoid DMT and other hallucinogens. DMT and ayahuasca have been linked to severe psychotic episodes, albeit this is an uncommon occurrence.

DMT is a fast-acting drug, but the method you use to

consume it impacts how quickly you feel its effects.

Intravenous injection: The effects emerge quickly, often instantly, and last for around 30 minutes.

Intramuscular injection: The effects appear in two to five minutes and last for around an hour.

Oral ingestion of ayahuasca tea: Effects begin after about an hour, peak in 90 minutes, and linger for about four hours.

Effects may show instantaneously and last less than 30 minutes if smoked or vaped. How Long Does DMT Keep You Awake?

The half-life of DMT is unknown, and it is thought to depend on how the drug is administered. The half-life of DMT injected is roughly 15 minutes, while DMT consumed in ayahuasca tea has a longer half-life.

DMT has little impact when taken orally because it is immediately broken down in the digestive tract by monoamine oxidase (MAO). The metabolites DMT-NO and IAA are produced during this process.

To be effective, an oral dose must be combined with a monoamine oxidase inhibitor (MAOI), which also has a prolonged impact. This is seen in ayahuasca tea, which contains an MAOI component derived from plants.

Standard drug tests used for law enforcement, employment, and therapy do not include DMT in the screening process. Specific testing is required to detect DMT in the blood, urine, hair, or saliva.

Blood

A blood test can only detect DMT for two hours after it is ingested.

A particular test would be required to identify it, and it would have to be done very fast after the drug was ingested.

Breath

There is no known DMT breath test.

Urine

For up to 24 hours after taking DMT, it can be identified in urine.

This necessitates the use of a particular test designed to detect hallucinogens such as DMT.

Hair

Hair tests can identify DMT and prove long-term drug use.7 Hair testing can detect drugs for up to 90 days after they've been consumed, though this figure varies depending on how frequently the substance is used.

Saliva

The length of time saliva tests can detect DMT is unknown. While most saliva tests cannot identify DMT after as little as one hour, research has shown that DMT can be detected in saliva samples four to twelve hours after consumption.

Factors Influencing Detection Time

Individual circumstances, such as the dosage consumed, can influence how long DMT stays in your system.

•The dosage taken

•Your weight

•Your age

•Your metabolism

•How frequently do you use the drug Smoking vs. Oral Ingestion

The way you take the medication may affect how long it stays in your system. DMT taken orally through ayahuasca tea or intramuscular injection may be less detectable than other methods. 3 Drug testing can detect DMT that has been smoked.

HOW TO REMOVE DMT FROM YOUR SYSTEM

There are no known methods for speeding up the metabolic process and getting DMT out of your system more quickly. Drinking extra water or eating a full meal won't help you get the drug out of your system faster; however, taking ayahuasca or another oral version of the drug on an empty stomach may.

Symptoms of Overdose

Overdosing on DMT is highly unusual and involves taking a very high amount of the substance. When combining DMT with other drugs, such as:

• A hazardous condition known as serotonin syndrome might ensue.

• Parkinson's disease is treated with levodopa.

- Lithium
- Triptans are migraine medicines.

SSRIs (selective serotonin reuptake inhibitors) are medications that prevent serotonin from being reabsorbed (SSRIs)

Serotonin syndrome can cause symptoms such as high fevers, loss of consciousness, seizures, and blood pressure or pulse changes.

If you or a loved one is suffering from serotonin syndrome, seek medical care as soon as possible.

Pregnant women should use caution as well. While the data in this area is inconclusive, animal studies have revealed that ayahuasca use can have detrimental consequences.

DMT, like most hallucinogens, is unlikely to be addictive, while the long-term effects of consistent usage are unknown. DMT tolerance does not appear to develop in regular users.

DMT consumption can lead to a terrible trip with unpleasant side effects such as intense anxiety and palpitations. DMT can impair judgment, leading to risky decisions, particularly for those who aren't used to the drug's effects.

Chapter 5: DMT EXTRACTION

Like the other well-known psychedelics LSD and psilocybin, DMT is a molecule that mimics the serotonin neurotransmitter. DMT's psychological effects are mediated through the 5-HT2A receptor, which is found mostly in parts of the brain associated with high-level cognition, such as self-awareness, emotions, and introspection.

DMT produces a brief, intense psychedelic experience when smoked or injected intravenously. Individuals have described the feeling as though they were ripped from their bodies and tossed across space at incredible speeds. DMT causes vivid visions and aural hallucinations of distant landscapes, secret dimensions, and godlike entities. It frequently causes users to engage in profound introspection, allowing them to review prior memories and gain a new perspective on life.

Ayahuasca, an old psychedelic drink used in traditional South American healing rites, can also contain DMT. This is a completely different sensation from smoked or injectable DMT, as it lasts several hours instead of minutes and frequently causes vomiting and diarrhea. Despite the unpleasant nature of the experience, ayahuasca has been connected to several therapeutic effects, including the treatment of depression.

I'd want to provide you step-by-step instructions on where to look for DMT-containing plants and how to extract this powerful psychedelic component for personal use.

Where can I locate plants that are high in DMT?

Although DMT is illegal everywhere, the legality of DMT-containing plants varies. Plants containing DMT can be obtained online in a variety of locations.

This DMT extraction guide is geared to Mimosa hostilis root bark, the most commonly purchased DMT-containing plant. It usually comes in the form of a coarse powder, as shown here:

Mimosa hostilis root bark can be purchased online from a variety of sellers, although it may not be able to be transported to your country due to DMT-containing plant restrictions:

•I'm not aware of any sites shipping M. hostilis to the United States at the moment, but keep an eye on this space for updates.

•If you live in Europe or the United Kingdom, this site will most likely transport

M. hostilis to you.

Although this instruction is for M. hostilis, the extraction should work with any DMT- containing organic material – you just need to adapt the amount of starting material to the amount of DMT found in the plant species you're using.

Psychotria Viridis, which is utilized in traditional ayahuasca preparations, is another popular DMT-containing plant. To indigenous peoples, it is also known as Chacruna.

You can cultivate your DMT-containing plants from seeds if you're patient, as seeds aren't always as tightly regulated as plants. Reed Canary Grass seeds, for example, are available online in several regions.

Keep a lookout for new DMT-containing plants because the market is continually changing.

EXTRACTION OF DMT

This is a brief description of how DMT extraction chemistry works.

The most common procedure is 'acid/base extraction,' which is also the most complicated. We've opted to demonstrate the the straight base' extraction approach, which is a little easier. The chemistry is summarized as follows:

Powdered DMT-rich plants are mixed with a base, most commonly sodium hydroxide (NaOH). DMT molecules float around in a base solution once the plant material is dissolved.

The DMT is extracted from the base solution in the next step. The simple answer is that the base solution is charged (polar), while the DMT molecules aren't (non-polar). When a non-polar solvent is added to a polar base solution, the DMT molecules are attracted out. This non-polar solvent (which now contains the DMT) separates from the remainder of the solution and creates a distinct layer.

The final step is to separate the DMT molecules from the non-polar solvent, which either evaporation or freezing can accomplish.

The chemistry of the "Straight to Base" extraction method is simplified.

A STEP-BY-STEP TUTORIAL TO EXTRACTING DMT

The DMT-nexus tek of Noman was used as inspiration.

Please read the guide thoroughly and understand it before attempting the process. INGREDIENTS

- Water

- Plants that contain DMT, such as Mimosa hostilis root bark
- Lies (granulated sodium hydroxide)
- VM&P Naphtha (if unavailable, 40-60 Petroleum Ether can be used)
- vinaigrette (for safely cleaning up Lye spills)

EQUIPMENT

- A blender or grinder capable of smashing ice
- Four collection jars (glass jelly/jam jars will suffice)
- A spatula made of rubber
- Filters for coffee
- Freezer
- Eyedropper
- Pipette
- Personal safety equipment includes a fume mask, goggles, and rubber gloves.
- A glass mixing jar with a wide mouth and a tight-fitting lid (approximately a liter or larger) (depending on how much plant material you are starting with)

EXTRACTING DMT FROM THE PLANT IN STEP 1

•Cut and mix the plant material until it's as fine as possible; use a mask to keep the powder from getting into your lungs.

•Slowly add a tablespoon of lye to your water in your mixing jar at a time, stirring until thoroughly dissolved. To create 50g Mimosa hostilis bark, combine 750ml water and 50g lye. NOTE: Lye is a chemical that should be handled with caution because it can cause chemical burns. Any spills can be cleaned up with vinegar.

•Put the powdered plant in the container, tighten the lid, shake thoroughly, and put away for about an hour.

EXTRACTING DMT FROM THE BASE SOLUTION IN STEP 2

•For every 50g Mimosa hostilis bark, pour 50ml naphtha into the mixing jar.

•Replace the lid on the mixing jar and stir steadily for about a minute, turning the jar over several times. It's best not to shake it because shaking it will make it difficult to separate the two layers afterward.

•Set the mixing jar just on the counter and wait is for two layers of the mixture to separate.

•Gently agitate the area a couple of times more.

•Once the layers have separated after your last agitation, insert the top (clear) layer into one of your collecting jars with your pipette. This is where your DMT will be found. Darker bottom layers should be avoided because they contain hazardous bacteria that you don't want to transmit.

•To remove every last trace of DMT from the base solution, fill the mixing jar with fresh naphtha and repeat the previous operations three times more.

•To extract the most DMT from the base solution, leave the last batch of naphtha in the mixing jar for a few days.

•Freeze all four of your collecting jars (which contain DMT in a naphtha solution).

EXTRACTING DMT FROM THE NAPHTHA

SOLUTION IN STEP 3

•Your DMT should have crystallized in your collecting jars after being frozen. To collect the DMT, strain the solutions using a coffee filter. The naphtha can be preserved and used again in the future.

•NOTE: Many people claim that after freezing, DMT crystals are not visible. They may be suspended in the naphtha and appear after the naphtha has been poured through the filters. However, if your freezer isn't cold enough, the crystals may take longer to form. To get a cooler temperature, you can leave your collection jars in the freezer for longer.

•Scrape every last drop of naphtha solution from the collection jars using your rubber spatula.

•Carefully arrange for your coffee filters to dry. Once dried, this DMT powder is ready to smoke, but it can be further refined in the optional step below.

•Many folks find their DMT adhering to the side of the jars; if your coffee filters don't have any crystals, peek inside the jars.

STEP 4: RECRYSTALLISATION OF DMT FOR FURTHER REFINEMENT

•Fill a small glass jar halfway with DMT powder.

•Place your solvent (naphtha or heptane) in a different glass container. For every gram of DMT powder, you'll need roughly 25ml of solvent.

•To heat the contents of both glass containers, carefully place them in a pan of boiling water. NOTE: DO NOT use a gas stove or maintain open flames near your solvent because it emits flammable vapors.

•Using an eyedropper, drip little amounts of your hot solvent into the DMT powder. Swirl the glass jar and add solvent until the DMT is completely dissolved. Use as little solvent as possible if at all possible.

•Remove the pan from the heat and allow it to cool to room temperature.

•Refrigerate the glass container containing dissolved DMT powder, which is now at room temperature.

- Place the container in the freezer for a few hours when it has cooled down.

- You can now use a coffee filter to filter out your refined DMT crystal. This procedure can be repeated to achieve even higher levels of purity.

THE SHORT VERSION ADAPTED

For those of you who don't want to see all those processes and just want to get your DMT out of your plant as soon as possible (without worrying about purity or yield), here's a quicker method:

INGREDIENTS

- Water

- Plants that contain DMT, such as Mimosa hostilis root bark

- Lye (granulated sodium hydroxide)

- VM&P Naphtha (if unavailable, 40-60 Petroleum Ether can be used)

- vinaigrette (for safely cleaning up Lye spills)

EQUIPMENT

- Large mixing bowl made of ceramic (5L)
- Personal protection: rubber gloves and safety goggles
- Masher for potatoes
- A large baking dish made of glass
- Jug with a large capacity for measuring (2L)
- Fan PROCEDURE
- Break up 400-500g of Mimosa hostilis root bark in a mixing bowl. Make sure the bark doesn't fill the dish more than halfway.

- Pour 200g lye into 2-3L water slowly. NOTE: Lye is a chemical that should be handled with caution because it can cause chemical burns. Any spills can be cleaned up with vinegar. Wear gloves and goggles to protect your eyes.
- In a mixing bowl, combine your lye solution and root bark. Allow an hour.
- Using your potato masher, combine and crush your root bark for 20-30 minutes.

- Stir add 250 mL naphtha for another 20-30 minutes in the bowl.

- Allow the solvent to rise to the top of the mixture for a few minutes.

- Pour this into your glass baking dish after removing the clear solvent layer on top. Any of the dish's lower, darker layers should be avoided.

- Blow air across the baking dish with your fan to evaporate the solvent.

- The leftover powder is your DMT, which you can inhale. How can I tell whether the DMT I've extracted is pure?

When you produce your own DMT, you have to worry about how well you followed the instructions. You may wind up with additional contaminants in your DMT powder if you employed low-quality ingredients or did a sloppy job (i.e., accidentally carried over some of the base solutions). Smoking can be rather uncomfortable.

There is a misconception that the color of DMT powder indicates its purity; however, the color of DMT powder is affected by several circumstances. It is generally safe to smoke powder white, yellow, red, or brown. If it's green or blue, it means something went wrong during the extraction process, and you should try again.

Guides to alternative extraction methods

Many extraction techniques, as previously indicated, involve an acid/base extraction process, which we haven't addressed here because the straight-to-base method is much easier. However, there are many tutorials on the DMT-nexus if you want to be thorough and try an acid/base extraction.

Information on safety

In most countries, DMT is prohibited. I don't believe in breaking the law or utilizing DMT in ways that aren't legal or customary. If you do decide to use DMT, do your homework on the effects and risks.

DMT is a potent psychedelic that must be used with caution. You should be aware of the best ways to prepare for and integrate a psychedelic experience.

Keep track of how much you're taking! A 15mg dose of smoked DMT powder is recommended for first-time users.

Make sure you understand the process before you start using these extraction guides. If you're using a DMT-containing plant other than Mimosa hostilis, make sure you're aware of the differences and adjust your strategy accordingly. Wear rubber gloves, safety goggles, and a dust mask if you're grinding up plant debris.

Avoid getting it on your skin when working with lye (sodium hydroxide), and always wear safety goggles. If you get it on your skin, wash it off with plenty of water (and, if available, vinegar to neutralize the lye). If it goes into your eye, rinse it out for at least 20 minutes with tap water before going to the doctor. If there is a lot of it spilled, neutralize it with vinegar before cleaning it up. Start slowly and thoroughly mixing the lye into the water.